St. Patrick's Day

St. Patrick's Day

by **Joyce K. Kessel**

pictures by **Cathy Gilchrist**

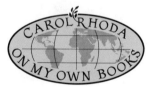

Carolrhoda Books • Minneapolis, Minnesota

LIBRARY OF CONGRESS CATALOGING IN PUBLICATION DATA

Kessel, Joyce.
  St. Patrick's Day.

  (A Carolrhoda on my own book)
  Summary: Presents a brief account of the
life of the Roman aristocrat who became
Ireland's patron saint and discusses the
annual holiday that honors him.
  1. St. Patrick's Day—Juvenile literature.
[1. Patrick, Saint 373?-463? 2. Saints.
3. St. Patrick's Day] I. Gilchrist, Cathy,
ill. II. Title. III. Title: Saint Patrick's
Day. IV. Series.
GT4995.P3K47   270.2′092′4 [B] [92]   82-1254
ISBN 0-87614-193-9   AACR2

    1 2 3 4 5 6 7 8 9 10 88 87 86 85 84 83 82

to Anne, Craig, and Ryan
—J.K.K.

to Peter Rochford Gilchrist
—C.G.

Saint Patrick's Day is March 17.
It is celebrated all over the world,
wherever there are people
of Irish background.
Some celebrate by wearing green.
Others celebrate by going to church.
Still others celebrate with parties.
Some cities even hold parades.
People have been celebrating
Saint Patrick's Day
for nearly 1600 years now.
It all began, of course,
with Saint Patrick himself.

Patrick is Ireland's patron saint.

He changed the history of Ireland,

and he is well loved

by the Irish people.

But Patrick was not born in Ireland.

He was born in England

between the years 372 and 390.

His parents did not even

name him Patrick!

We think they named him "Maewyn."

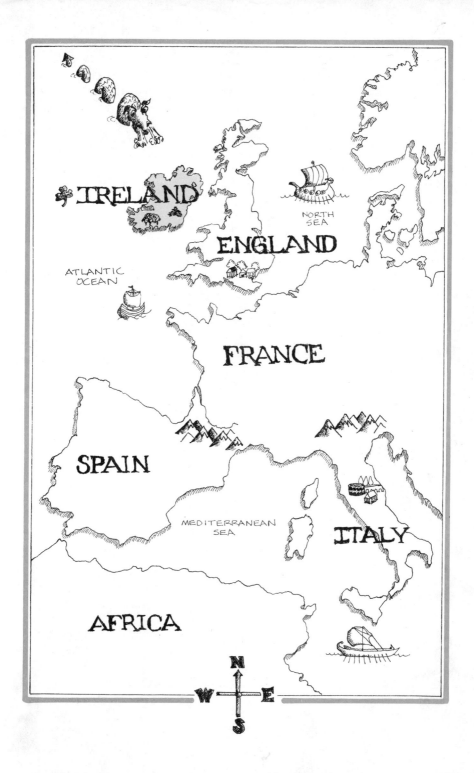

Patrick's parents were Romans.

At that time,

the Romans ruled England.

Roman cities in England had shops,

churches, and beautiful houses.

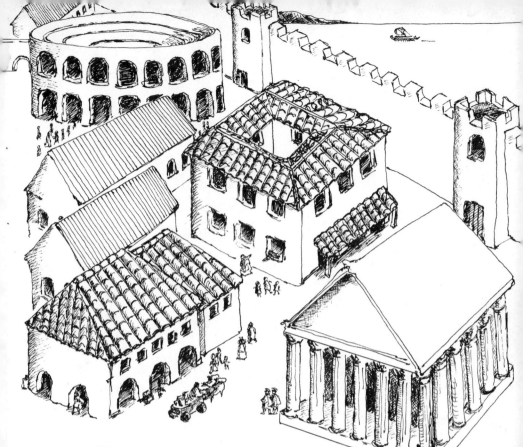

People read books.

They dressed in fine cloth gowns.

Calphurnius, Patrick's father,

was a high Roman official,

so Patrick lived a rich

and comfortable life.

But just across the Irish Sea,
in Ireland,
life was not so comfortable.

People lived in mud huts.

They dressed in animal skins.

They could not read.

Ireland was called Eire
in those days.
The Romans did not rule Eire.
It was ruled by tribal kings
who would not let the Romans in.
The Irish did not like the Romans.
They did not like
the Roman religion either.
The Irish believed in other gods.
They did not want to become
Christians like the Romans.

15

When Patrick was a boy,
the most powerful king in Ireland
was named Niall.
In the year 400,

King Niall attacked England.

He took thousands of prisoners.

He wanted them for slaves.

Patrick was one of them!

Patrick was taken to
northern Ireland.
There he was sold to another king,
named Meliucc.

The rich little Roman boy
was forced to herd pigs and sheep.
After a fine, rich life,
Patrick became a swineherd.

Meliucc and his family
were not unkind to Patrick.
Meliucc's children were good company.
There was plenty of food.
Still, Patrick was only 15 years old.
He was all alone in a strange land.
He didn't know the language.
He didn't even know
if his family was still alive.
There were no beautiful houses,
no shops, no books.
Patrick slept in a mud hut.

He was only a little slave boy
far from home.

At first, Patrick was frightened.

Then he became filled

with a great sadness.

He began to think and dream

all the time.

He began to sleep outdoors.

Only rocks protected him

from the winter wind.

Like the sheep,

he didn't seem to feel it.

Like the pigs,

he roamed the valleys.

He prayed day and night,

and his prayers seemed to

protect him from the cold.

The little slave boy became
one of the great religious dreamers
of all time.
Soon he began to have
wonderful dreams.

The dreams told him to escape.
One day Meliucc's children
could not find him.
The animals were astray.
The slave boy was gone.

Patrick was then about 21 years old.

After six years as a slave,

he had run away.

He walked many miles to the sea.

There he found a ship.

It took him back to England.

But he was not ready

for what he found.

His country was in ruins!

The Romans had been chased out.

They were no longer the rulers.

It is said that Patrick then
wandered all through Europe.
Everywhere he found the same thing.
The Romans had been chased out.
Then, in the year 410,
the mighty city of Rome—
the center of all Roman power—
was conquered as well.
To Patrick, it was like
the end of the world.
His past was really dead.
He had nowhere to go.
His God sent him no more dreams.

29

Though it was dangerous,
Patrick decided to go back
to England.
He lived very quietly there.
All he did was pray and think.

One day another voice
came to him. It said,
"Holy youth, we beg thee to come
and walk once more among us."

Patrick was certain that God
was calling him back to Ireland.
Wild Ireland!
Land of magical mists and green!
Patrick had almost forgotten it.
Now he remembered the beautiful land
and how much he had loved the people.
It all came back like a spell.
Suddenly Patrick knew
what he was supposed to do.
He was supposed to bring
all those tribes together.
He was supposed to make
Ireland a Christian land.
Patrick was sure of it.

But first there was work to do.

Patrick went to France.

For the next ten years,

he studied religion there.

During all that time,

he thought of Ireland.

He never forgot

the voice in the dream.

In the year 432, Pope Celestine

made Patrick a bishop.

The pope named him "Patricius."

Patricius is the Latin word for "Patrick."

Now at last, Bishop Patrick
sailed for Ireland.
But his mission was not easy.
The Irish people turned him away.
They tried to stone him to death.

Patrick and his men
fled to the sea again.
Some time later,
they returned to shore.
They found a barn
and went to sleep there.

The barn belonged to a king
named Dichu.
Dichu thought Patrick and his men
were robbers.
He wanted to kill them.
But when he saw Patrick,
Dichu could not move.
Patrick held out his hand and smiled.
Something wonderful shone in his face.
Dichu put down his weapon.
Even his fierce dog stopped growling.
(It may not have happened
exactly like that,
but that is how the story
has been told.)

Dichu became the first Christian
in Ireland.

His barn became the first church.

Not everyone in Ireland

was happy to have Patrick back.

There were many people

who hated Patrick's religion.

They stoned Patrick.

Once they even put him in chains.

But Patrick always escaped.

He traveled all over Ireland.

The stories say

he always had a drummer with him.

When he came to a village,

the drummer would drum,

and the people would come running

from their houses.

Then they would listen to him.

Patrick talked about one God.

This seemed strange

to the Irish people.

They had always believed

in many gods.

Patrick showed them a shamrock.

A shamrock is like
a three-leafed clover.
Then Patrick explained the idea
of the Father, Son, and Holy Spirit.
Today the shamrock is
Ireland's national flower.

More and more people
were becoming Christians.
More and more Irish kings
were becoming Christians too.
As they came together to worship,
the Irish people began
to come together as a country too.
Patrick built hundreds of churches
in Ireland.
He spent the rest of his life
watching over them.
When he died on March 17,
between the years 461 and 492,
the church buried him
at Downpatrick in Ireland.

The church also made him a saint.
Patrick had lived out his dream.
Ireland had become
one country under one god.

There are many legends
about Saint Patrick.
It is said that he got rid
of all the snakes in Ireland.
By beating his drums,
he frightened them into the sea.
It is said that he raised
his father from the dead.
They say that people
fed Patrick poison,
but he did not die.
They say that Patrick
could make snow burn.

They say that the sun would not set
when Patrick died.
It shone in the sky
for twelve days and nights.
It would not make a new day
without him.

They say that the fish
rise from the sea each March 17.
They pass before Patrick's altar,
then disappear.

Saint Patrick's Day has become
a holiday in both the U.S. and Canada.
It is a day of fun and parties.
But March 17 is more serious
in Ireland.

There is some singing and dancing,
but for most Irish people
it is a holy time.
People fill the churches
for three days.

The first Saint Patrick's Day
in North America
was held in Boston in 1737.
Now there are parades
in many large cities.
Thousands of people find some way
to celebrate Saint Patrick's Day.
Some only wear green.
Some also dance and sing Irish songs.

But wherever Irish people may be,
they feel a little homesick
on March 17.
A few tears mix with their laughter.
Wild jigs change into sad songs,
and back again.
Others feel the sadness and the joy.
They want to be part of it.
On Saint Patrick's Day,
almost everyone seems to be
a little bit Irish.

About the Author

Joyce K. Kessel is the author of two other ON MY OWN books, HALLOWEEN, which was a 1981 Children's Choice, and VALENTINE'S DAY. Ms. Kessel was born and grew up in North Dakota. For eleven years she worked as a speech therapist and school administrator in Puerto Rico, but she now makes her home in Minneapolis.

About the Artist

Cathy Gilchrist is no stranger to ON MY OWN books either. She illustrated I NEVER WIN! by Judy Delton, a 1982 Children's Choice. Ms. Gilchrist holds a B.F.A. in drawing and painting from the University of Minnesota as well as a B.A. in French. She lives in St. Paul with her ten-year-old son, Jeremy.